This Book Belongs To

_____

Jackson and the Big Blue Boots

by **Mary Jane Kooiman**

illustrated by Rick Cunningham

Once there was a little boy
Who lived across the street,
A carefree kid named Jackson
Who never saw his feet!

It didn't matter what the weather.

It didn't matter where he was going.

It could be hot or cold or windy.

It might even be snowing!

He wore boots!

He wore boots!

He wore big blue boots!

Oh! How Jackson loved his big blue boots!

He was never seen without them.

He wore them all day every day.

His big blue boots matched everything.

"They look just fine," he'd say.

He wore them while climbing trees.

He wore them running in the park.

He wore them when the sun was shining,

And he wore them in the dark.

He wore boots!

He wore boots!

He wore big blue boots!

Oh! How Jackson loved his big blue boots!

He wore them when he was swinging

And when going down the slide.

He wore them in the sandbox

And when on his bike he'd ride.

He wore them when he was reading.

He wore them playing games.

He wore them playing baseball.

He wore boots!

He wore boots!

He wore big blue boots!

Oh! How Jackson loved his big blue boots!

He wore them on the school bus.
They made him feel so lucky.

He wore them in the bathtub
With his favorite rubber ducky!

He wore them in the country.

He wore them in the city.

He wore them when he was playing
With his puppy and his kitty.

He wore them eating breakfast.

He wore them sleeping in his bed.

He wore them doing everything,
Even standing on his head!

He wore boots!

He wore boots!

He wore big blue boots!

Oh! How Jackson loved his big blue boots!

One day he looked at those big blue boots,
And that day he changed his mind
About his boots and lots of things,
And he left those boots behind.

Jackson knew he didn't want

To wear them anymore.

He put on his tennis shoes

And walked right out the door!

He walked to his favorite store.

He smiled and that was that.

He looked in the window and said,

"I think I like that big red hat!"

The End

Made in the USA
Lexington, KY
07 June 2010